MOUNTAIN

and

molehills

Poetry

of

Michael Gordon Dickson

Copyright © 2013 Michael Gordon Dickson

All rights reserved

ISBN-13:978-1482028843
    -10: 1482028840

DEDICATION

For my son, Sean and my daughter, Holly and in memory of my mother, who taught me the meaning of love.

With an impossible debt of thanks to my very special friend and mentor, Janet, who manages to combine proof reader, driving force and "Thomas" all into one remarkable person.

Author's Note

Should you be able to find even one from this miscellany of verse that prompts you to smile, think, laugh, or cry then please know that you have made any effort on my part worthwhile.

Table of contents

A TOAST 10

CHILDREN OF MANKIND.............................12

NO CONSIDERATION FOLK..........................14

ME OR YOU..16

HOW TO RAISE A PSYCHOPATH 18

RIPPLES IN THE STREAM............................21

BE TRUE TO YOURSELF...............................23

THOMAS 24

NO CREATURES GREAT AND SMALL 26

LET IT GO 28

IT'S NOT FAIR...30

LOST 32

HALF EMPTY CUP 33

LOVE THY NEIGHBOUR................................34

LONELINESS, THY MANTLE	35
LADY LUCK	37
THE GOLDEN YEARS	38
THE GARDEN OF EDEN	40
YOU WERE A MAN	42
PURSUIT OF EXCELLENCE	44
SELF DIAGNOSIS	46
PREHISTORIC JOY	47
HOLD ON TO YOUR DREAM	49
GOD'S GREATEST GIFT	51
TABLE FOR TWO	53
JOCK	55
FOUR LETTER WORD	57
HEAVEN ON EARTH	58
SINS OF THE FATHERS	61
IF YOU ASK ME	62

EVE'S APPLE...63

ONCE I WAS..65

SECURITY CONSCIOUS 67

PEARLY GATES..69

PANDORA'S BOX..70

A GRAIN OF SAND..72

ANOTHER CLICHE..74

HOLLY 76

WELL- BALANCED VIEW 77

JIGSAW 79

PEOPLE AND ONIONS 81

FIRST THOUGHTS..83

FAITH, HOPE AND CHARITY 84

LADY IN THE HOUSE 88

THE GOOD OLD DAYS 89

ANGEL...91

SANCTUARY	93
WINDOWS OF THE SOUL	95
HOW ARE YOU?	97
A FATHER'S PRAYER	98
MESSAGE TO OUTER SPACE	100
A FRIEND IN NEED	102
I WILL SERVE THE WINE	103
ONE OF THOSE DAYS	105
THE CHILD IN YOUR EYES	106
MY PRIZE	107
BRAIN SCAN	108
BROTHER ASS	110
MASTERMIND	114
FAMOUS LAST WORDS	116
EUREKA	117
THINGS	119

REMEMBER ME 121

I AM MAN..122

WITHOUT YOU 124

POET'S BLOCK 125

A TOAST

To the land of tartan and of bagpipes
Land of auld lang syne
Land of haggis and of whisky
Land that God made mine.
Land of lochs and purple heather
Land of misty morning glen
Land of stone built castles
That saw deeds beyond our ken.
Land of stag up on the hillside
Land of eagle in the sky
Land of Loch Ness depths
Where Nessie's secrets lie.
Land of Edinburgh Castle
Majestic on a rock so steep
Land of Bruce's spider
Land of Rob Roy's leap.
Land of great inventors
Advanced before their time
Land of Rabbie Burns
And poetry sublime.
Land of the auld course at St. Andrews
Land of ceilidh nights
Land of Greyfriar's Bobby
Land of Northern lights.
Land of Scott and land of Stevenson

Land of music and the arts
Land of William Wallace,
The bravest of all hearts.
Land that fought with valour
In the name of liberty
Land that gave me birth
I raise my glass to thee.

CHILDREN OF MANKIND

There's a sound in the distance
Which speaks of our fate.
Has it caught our attention
Or have we left it too late?
It's the sound of men with chainsaws
Cutting forests to the bone.
It's the sound of birds and animals
Crying for their home.
It's the sound of zealots praying
As they lay another mine.
It's the sound of politicians
Saying "Everything is fine."
It's the sound of trawler engines
As they empty all our seas.
It's the sound of gas escaping
From a million factories.
It's the sound of rich men raging
When their market takes a dive.
It's the sound of babies crying
With no food to stay alive.
It's the sound of bombs exploding
To prove somebody wrong.
It's the sound of barren silence
As the songbird ends his song.

It's the sound of mothers weeping
For the world they'll leave behind,
With so many implications
For the children of mankind.

NO CONSIDERATION FOLK

These no consideration folk
Have really got beyond a joke.
This world would be a better place
Without my fellow human race.
They only think of number one
With no concern for anyone.
Why, only just the other day
A blind man wandered in my way.
His trainee guide dog was a pup.
It very nearly tripped me up!
If that was not enough to stand
A strange old lady took my hand
And asked for help to cross the road.
I told her "Read the highway code!
And here's a hint to keep you right,
Take a look at that green light."
Back home I sat on my settee
And settled down to watch T.V.
A charity pest knocked on my door.
I gave last year, she's back for more.
I made it plain as plain could be
I didn't own a money tree.
And by the time I watched her go
I'd missed my favourite T.V. Show!

Lord, no consideration folk
Have really got beyond a joke
To see how selfish folk can be.
Lord, you must be pleased with me.

ME OR YOU

Is it me
Or is it you?
Are you wrong
And am I right?
Is this leading to an argument
Or heading for
A fight?
Is it you
Or is it me?
We can't see
Eye to eye.
Temperatures are rising.
Emotions
Getting high.
I don't know
If it's me.
I don't know
If it's you.
I only know that suddenly
I've changed my
Point of view.
It may be you.
It may be me.
But this isn't worth

The fuss.
Let me hold you
In my arms
For all that matters is
It's us.

HOW TO RAISE A PSYCHOPATH

You could show them "Chainsaw Massacre",
Perhaps when they are four
Or "Nightmare Down in Elm Street"
Might unhinge them even more.
But start about the age of two
To get a slow decline
And the blueprint to success is
The book of nursery rhyme.
The best time to begin is
When your child is tucked in bed,
With darkness slowly falling,
You can get inside their head.
Two horrific accidents
Will stop things being dull.
A man called Jack, falls down a hill
And fractures his skull.
And with an egg called Humpty
Deep sadness will be found
When he falls off a wall
And is scrambled on the ground.
A kid called Willie Winkie
Can provoke copycat traumas
By running through the streets at night
Dressed only in pyjamas.

And sexual harassment
Is important to instill,
So read them Georgie Porgie
Which exactly fits the bill.
Cruelty to animals
Must not be left behind,
The story is essential
Of the three mice who are blind.
Just when you think this classic
Might be going off the rails,
A woman with a knife appears
And cuts off their tails.
A rewarding look of horror
You will see in your child's eye,
When you discuss the details
Of the "Blackbirds in a Pie."
But save the very best till last,
Repeat it every night.
It's guaranteed to leave your child
In deep, psychotic fright.
A madman steals a cradle
With a baby tucked inside,
He puts it up a tree
Then he finds place to hide.
He calls up to the baby
Saying "Husha" and Bye-byes".
A howling gale then snaps a branch
And so the baby dies.
And that's the time to say "Sleep well"

And then turn out the light,
And leave your horror-stricken child
To its nightmare plight.
Now you deserve a glass of wine,
Relaxing in a bath
And toast yourself for starting
To raise a psychopath.

RIPPLES IN THE STREAM

A stone is dropped in water
And ripples swell and glide.
Not ours to know
How far they flow
In their outward tide.
And likewise, every action
Bears consequence unseen.
All that we say
And that we do
Leave ripples in the stream.
A lie in gossip spoken
Incurs a toxic gain.
It journeys on
Till faith is gone
In someone's once good name.
And a single act of malice
With the victim, does not die.
For those who care,
That grief will share
The pain will multiply.
And what may be the yield
Of a smile or outstretched hand?
That gesture could mean so much more
Than we might understand.

An act of selfless love
With the loved one
Does not part.
In years ahead, that gift, long given
Lives to warm a lonely heart.
So though you conclude your action
And draw an end to what you've said
It's just the end
Of the beginning
As the ripples start to spread.

BE TRUE TO YOURSELF

Be true to yourself.
Do not self deceive.
Respect others views
For what they believe.
Be slow to anger.
Be quick to smile.
Be honest and open.
Never hide behind guile.
When you have success,
Give others their due
And say to misfortune,
"Is that the best you can do?"
Be ready to give
Rather than take.
Keep your heart open,
Even though it might break.
Walk your own path
With a purposeful stride.
Be aware, fame and fortune
Are ambitions of pride.
Lend your strength to the weak.
Take sides with the few.
Stand up and be counted.
To yourself be true.

THOMAS

From being born into a world
Of endless questions
At zero starting point
First truths you could reveal.
If you could touch it or could eat it
If you could hear it and repeat it
And you could see it,
Then you knew that it was real.
But Thomas, rules of infancy
Are what you cling to
And to what you cannot see
You still are blind.
For you must see it to believe it
Or repudiate and leave it
And you have pulled the shutters down
Around your mind.
And Thomas, three score years and ten
Are all we're given
For the meaning of our life
To be attained.
So do not live in chains of doubt
And rule a quest for knowledge out
For if eternal life exists
It must be gained.

And one day, everyone
Must put their faith in something
And let their spirit lead them
Deaf and blind.
And if the cynics are betrayed
When that leap of faith is made,
Will you then be
The doubting Thomas
Left behind?

NO CREATURES GREAT AND SMALL

You couldn't marvel at a lion
With his majestic mane of fur
And your heart would not be warmed
To hear a kitten purr.
And you would never smile
To hear a parrot mimic us
Or to hear a small child, try to say,
Hippopotamus.
You would not see an elephant,
Kangaroo or chimpanzee.
There'd be no image of a teddy bear
In your nursery.
You could not laugh at a monkey.
There'd be no horse to ride.
You'd never know the loyalty
A dog gives at your side.
No pets to teach our children
How to love
And how to care.
And for all those lonely people,
No companionship to share.
What an empty world to live in
With no animals at all,
If man lived on his own

With no creatures great and small.
So if you're visiting the zoo
Or just dog-walking in the park,
Say a silent, "Thank You"
To Noah and his ark.

LET IT GO

Let it go.
Let it fly.
Consign it to the wind.
Release your soul from memories that weep.
Discard the mask of tragic clown.
Unlock the chains that hold you down.
Precious moments are the only ones to keep.
You have been hurt
Or been betrayed
Or been forsaken
And the joy of love and life
Is what is taken.
And the longer you give in
That thief will calculate a win
But if you free your heart
He is mistaken.
For if you cling to desolation
Like a prize
It will suffocate your dreams
And dim your eyes.
So raise your head
And see the stars
And you will know
That you have so much life to live,
And you have so much left to give.

Let it fade.
Let it die.
Let it go.

IT'S NOT FAIR

He entered this world,
As the record book shows,
So fit and so healthy,
Ten fingers, ten toes.
And in the next bed
Was a mother, beguiled,
With a tear in her eye
For her handicapped child.
The first boy grew up
Getting stronger each day,
But never liked problems
Coming his way.
Injustice, it seemed,
Was exclusive to him.
Only he, was exposed
To lady luck's whim.
He became pessimistic
And weighed down with care.
A day never passed
Without "It's not fair".
And as he grew older
People left him alone,
Wrapped up in self pity,
He seldom left home.

He might have done better
Had it entered his head,
To think of the child
Born in the next bed.

LOST

My va va voo has lost an m.
My mo has lost its jo.
My pizz has lost an azz.
My libid has lost an o.
My char has lost an m.
My pres has lost an ence.
My savoire's lost its faire.
My common's lost its sense.
My strong has lost its ox.
My broad has lost its back.
My fit has lost its fiddle.
My six has lost its pack.
My head has lost some hair.
My sure has lost its touch.
My smile has lost a tooth.
I don't use the mirror much.
My charis has lost a ma.
My personal has lost ity.
If I carry on like this
There won't be much left of me.
And if this is getting old
Then I'm duly not impressed.
But I won't lose myself
I've got my name sewn on my vest.

HALF EMPTY CUP

If you have a half full cup
Then you're always going to try.
You will overcome life's problems
Not let them pass you by.
A smile is your companion.
A stranger is a frown.
For you, the only way is up.
There's no road leading down.
You will know times of great sadness
When your spirits need a lift
But you always will appreciate
That life's your greatest gift.
But if your cup's half empty
There's no point to it all.
Each time you turn a corner
You hit another wall.
Most people have good fortune
While it by-passes you
And they don't have an inkling
Of what you're going through.
And your cup remains half empty
As you trudge life's weary road.
You failed to see it was so full
That it had overflowed.

LOVE THY NEIGHBOUR

You don't wear your hair the same as me.
Your skin's not fair the same as me
And you don't dress the same as me,
Not more or less the same as me.
I find your appearance so weird
And you have a very strange beard.
You don't say the things I do
Or even pray the way I do.
You don't adhere to things I do
And don't hold dear the things I do.
And your habits and culture I find
Too alien for my peace of mind.
You don't drink the same as me
And you don't think the same as me.
You don't cook the same as me.
No holy book the same as me.
So there's only two paths
We can take.
We'll make war
For our differences sake
Or – our differences
We understand
And we smile
As we hold out our hand.

LONELINESS, THY MANTLE

Loneliness, thy mantle fits me well,
More than I would ever want to tell.
But as a guest, you're uninvited.
Your attentions unrequited.
I have no wish to buy
From what you sell.
Loneliness, I know too well thy goal.
Your master has bequeathed to you, your role.
From stagnant shadows of the gloom
You will creep into my room
And drain the very essence of my soul.
And your choice of victim tells of what you are.
The elderly and weak you choose to scar
And you will whisper in their ear
Of things that no one wants to hear
Then watch in satisfaction from afar.
And your entrance turns a smile into a frown
And a once buoyant human nature
You will drown.
For solitaire's your game
And you leave them halt and lame
With the only road you show them
Leading down.
But loneliness, my dark, deceptive friend,

That is a road
That you will not make me descend.
I know that somewhere deep within me
I have one good fight left in me
And our relationship has now come to an end.
For in my solitude, my memories can flow
And fill my heart with warm and rosy glow.
I'll walk in dear, remembered places
With precious, loving faces.
So close the door behind you
As you go.

LADY LUCK

He fell off a cliff
Where he hung by a thread
But a chance passer-by
Pulled him back from the dead.
He was digging his garden
When he struck gold.
Those old Roman coins
Made a fortune I'm told.
He ran down the platform
And narrowly failed
To get on a train
That then got de-railed.
When he ran out of cash
To pay any bill
He was left fifty thousand
From a great uncle's will.
In the woods one day walking
There came a loud crack
A branch fell and flattened
A man five yards back.
He should have been bankrupt.
He should have been dead.
Then he ran out of luck
And got married instead.

THE GOLDEN YEARS
(FOR SEAN)

Once, I was eighteen
With my life's road to tread.
The world lay at my feet
With my golden years ahead.
Once, I had ambition
To see what I could do,
To calculate a gamble,
To take a risk or two.
And once, the mirror showed me
A young man in his prime
And pretty girls then seemed disposed
To share a little time.
I fell in love, I bought a ring
Promotion came my way
And the sound of children's laughter
Soon filled a summer's day.
Once, life was so fulfilling
Yet, with the passing time
I reached the summit of life's hill
And started the decline.
But this is how life must be
When all is said and done.
The pretty girls respect me now
While they smile at my son.
And now he is eighteen
Bereft of doubts or fears

My heart says son, it's your turn,
Go embrace those golden years.

THE GARDEN OF EDEN

The Garden of Eden,
Where man first said,
"I am."
A place where the lion
Lay down with the lamb.
Where man was one with nature
And had done no wrong,
In harmony bound
With the lark's joyful song.
Where no creatures were frightened
To see him pass by
And the tiger walked with him
With content in its eye.
With bountiful fruit trees
Yielding more than their worth
And a cycle of life
In a warm fertile earth.
Where the sun knew no winter.
Clouds gave gentle rain.
Stars shone down from heaven
And the world knew no pain.
No heartbroken tears.
No souls in despair.
No disease and no hunger.

No battlefields there.
No factory fumes, no traffic din.
No lies, no deception.
No aggression.
No sin.
Paradise lost...
And if it were so
And this was our birthright,
Why did we let it go?

YOU WERE A MAN

He came to my cradle
When my life began
And my father said "Son,
One day you'll be a man."
And he gave me no rule book
In the years that I grew
But to emulate him
Was all I had to do.
When we laid him to rest,
It was so clear to me,
My father's son
Was what I must be.
I must be firm but gentle
Be kind but be strong
Defend what is right
And reject what is wrong.
Put others first
In all that I do.
Be honest and faithful
And steadfast and true.
I would need a strong shoulder
For the lame to lean on
And be willing to fight
When all hope was gone.

And I know that I've done
The best I could do
To walk in his shadow
My whole life through.
And when my life is ended
I pray that I can
Hear my father say,
"Son, you were a man."

PURSUIT OF EXCELLENCE

A world of make believe, you might imagine,
No longer in pursuit of excellence.
With arts downgraded in a time
Devoid of melody and rhyme,
Artistic merit relegated by pretence.
Where, in a gallery you'd come across a painting
Displaying blots and coloured streaks
Both straight and bent,
While a critic in bow tie
With rapture in his eye
Would claim to see just what the artist meant.
Popular music they'd evaluate by decibel
With constant repetition of one line
And when the act was through
An ovation would ensue
To acclaim a live performance that was mimed.
And the Bible, the Koran and works of Shakespeare
In the literary world you would not see
But every bookshop would have queues
To buy the book in all the news-
The rise to fame of a "Z" list celebrity.
You would be told that all these works
Were works of legends
And poetry that rhymed was so last year

And comedy could only please
When it had crossed all boundaries
And silk purses could be made from a pig's ear.
Let us be thankful not to live in such a world
With only mirrors and illusions to be had
But be aware day is not night
And black is never white.
For whom the gods wish to destroy
They first make mad.

SELF DIAGNOSIS

With half an hour to kill
I took a book down from the shelf.
A "Medical Companion"
Which was all about good health.
I got to page eleven
Then something caught my eye,
With the symptoms there for jaundice
I could identify.
I told myself don't worry
And keep a sense of humour.
That worked 'till I discovered
That I'd got a bladder tumour.
I found out I had thrombosis,
Listeriosis, psittacosis
And the signs all indicated
That I'd got tuberculosis
And sinusitis and sceritis
And osteomilitis,
Tendonitis, meningitis
And acute peritonitis.
I staggered to the table
As my eyes began to fill
And said a silent prayer
As I sat and wrote my will.

PREHISTORIC JOY

In their animal skins,
In our ancestral caves,
The womenfolk waited
The return of their braves.
The men folk, out hunting
Would soon be back in,
With a deer on their backs,
To feed all their kin.
Then the women looked out
As they heard the sound
Of their menfolk all singing
And dancing around,
Whooping and laughing
And hugging each other,
Father to son,
And brother to brother.
The womenfolk stared
At each man and boy,
Thinking, "We see no food,
So why all this joy?"
"No food?" said the women
Almost too scared to mention,
As the men all cried out,
"We've made an invention!"

One brave woman spoke,
"So what's the big deal?
To bring no food home,
Have you invented the wheel?"
The head man replied proudly,
"No food so you say ? No,
But men down the ages,
Will remember this day.
So be quiet, silly woman,
You know nothing at all.
Today is the day,
Man invented the ball!"

HOLD ON TO YOUR DREAM

Hold on to your dream
Wherever it flies.
Let it strengthen your heart
And keep the child in your eyes.
Shelter it well
From each oncoming storm.
Keep the flame burning,
Keep it constant and warm.
There's a path for the lonely
To walk in this life,
Through bereavement, injustice
And heartbreak and strife.
And that path may be twisting
And uphill and long.
Hold on to your dream.
Let it keep your will strong.
For the spirit that faded
In the dead of the night
Might have awakened
To a life changing light.
And that corner to turn,
As hard as it may seem,
May be hiding the key
To fulfilling your dream.

So throw a coin in the fountain.
Wish on a star.
We all need our dream
Whoever we are.

GOD'S GREATEST GIFT

In my life, I have known sadness
And she certainly knows me
And she's taken me to places
That I didn't want to be.
And she has a companion
Called depression, who's as bad,
And together they can undermine
What will you've ever had.
But you have a choice of weapons
To make this twosome flee.
There's philosophy and faith
And humour makes it three.
Perhaps, you may have faith
To build a defence wall.
With faith you may be able
To make sense of it all.
But failing that, philosophy
May drive away your curse.
Take a good long look around you,
You'll see someone who is worse.
But if you're close to surrender,
There's one weapon left to lift.
It is a panacea
And it is god's greatest gift.

Your demons will fly swiftly
And will take the shortest path
To get away from hearing
That you still know how to laugh.

TABLE FOR TWO

Each year on your birthday
We knew what we'd do,
Your favourite bistro
And a table for two.
I knew what you'd say
As we came through their hall
"I do love that painting
That hangs on their wall."
And no matter the years
That we'd sat here to dine
We'd laugh and we'd talk
Over each glass of wine.
And the bustle around us
Would fade and would die
'Till the only ones there
Were just you and I.
And I'd look at your sweet face
And laughter- filled eyes
Thinking what did I do
To deserve such a prize.
And life is so special
With someone to share
But those we love most
Can't always be there.

Happy birthday, my darling,
The painting deal's done!
Look, it's on the spare chair
At my table for one.

JOCK

Deep in the past, he roamed the hills
Of this God given land.
The heather knew his footstep,
The lochs, his thirst-cupped hand.
His kilted stride would lead him
Across terrain bestowed at birth
And with all that he beheld,
He gloried in its worth.
He saw the mountains and the glens.
He marvelled at the northern lights,
Misty forests, rushing rivers
And star encrusted nights.
The silhouette of noble stag
Against a twighlit sky
And the salmon leaping upstream,
Would see him passing by
And his bed was of pine needles,
A rippling burn, his lullaby
And the shadow of an eagle
Would pass over where he'd lie.
And all that filled his eyes
Would his heart and spirit lift
And he knelt upon the heather
And gave thanks for such a gift.

No monuments now honour him
No statues, towers or cairns.
Yet he lives within our hearts
For we're a' Jock Tamson's bairns

FOUR LETTER WORD

There's a four letter word
Which you hear every day.
It has got four letters
And ends in a "K".
I hear it from strangers
And people I know.
It's driving me mad
Wherever I go.
And they say "Get away to --", and
"Get to blank, blank."
It's high time to end it.
We need a think tank
To devise a new word
To appear on the scene,
That isn't disgusting,
Offensive, obscene.
Let's all make an effort
To eliminate
This horrible word
That I have grown to hate.
I would be so happy.
It would be such a perk
If I never again
Heard that awful word – work.

HEAVEN ON EARTH

From a place of divine love
And perfect grace
A soul was sent to cross the great divide
To bear the weight of human life
In this world of tears and strife
And at the moment of his birth
The baby cried.
And for a while the child recalled
From whence he came
But the challenge of this world
Had to be met.
So the code of life began
Of how to grow and be a man
But something in his heart
Could not forget.
And with childhood left behind
He saw his brothers
Pursue the riches of this world
At costly price
And take the best this life can give
So that they might live
In their shallow memory
Of paradise.
His back then turned on earthly acquisition

And a path of self denial was his way
And his vocation then began
To serve his fellow man,
For he was led by what his heart
Still had to say.
To the sick he gave his love
And his compassion.
To the poor he gave whatever he could give.
His strength upheld the meek
And his arms held up the weak.
His noble heart had chosen
How he was to live.
And the privileged looked down
From latticed windows
As the maid turned back the sheets
Upon their beds.
For years, they watched him down below
As he hurried to and fro
Helping others
And they smiled and shook their heads.
But came the day when he had given
All he had
And his body fell and lay there in the rain
And they found him where he lay
And many knelt to pray
As his spirit journeyed back
From whence it came.
And the great and good stood back
And were dumbfounded

When thousands came to mourn
In tribute to his worth,
For how would they have known
To all those people, he had shown
The kind of love that spoke of
Heaven on this earth.

SINS OF THE FATHERS

I will teach my son to hate them,
Despise their race, blaspheme their creed,
So that when he is a man
My prejudice will breed.
And I will justify my bias
As my father did before
And tell of long forgotten conflict
When two tribes went to war.
And he will grow to wear our colours
And sing our songs of hate,
Then I will look on him with pride,
And we will celebrate.
For we must guard each generation
Compliance must be banned
For it could be that in their ignorance
They take an outstretched hand.
And when my life is ended
I will know my work is done
Ensuring sins of the fathers
Are visited on the sons.

IF YOU ASK ME

"Did you hear that Jenny's pregnant,
Though she hasn't said a word
But I heard it from Marie,
Who heard it from a little bird.
I saw Jean and Mr. Burns
At the club the other night
And they seemed very friendly,
If you take my meaning right.
And you know that Irish couple
Moved in next to Ann and Chris?
They've got a heated greenhouse.
They'll be growing cannabis.
Now, I'm not one to gossip
Or to speak of what I see
But Linda McAvennie's
Had botox, if you ask me.
You know Gerry Green was fired.
Well, I speak in pure detachment
But it's my belief he got the sack
For sexual harassment."
It's the same in every high street
And in all the earth's dominion,
Minimum information
Leads to maximum opinion.

EVE'S APPLE

Eve was the first,
Perhaps the worst.
Her apple, Adam's bubble burst
With "Taste it,
A shame to waste it."
And through the ages it's the same.
She holds the cards,
Controls the game.
He chases.
She holds the aces.
The Queen of Sheba and Helen of Troy
Used their charms in a devious ploy.
Lady Godiva and Delilah and Salome
Could make any boy
Their toy.
And nature laughs at man.
It's a part of god's eternal plan.
Let's face it.
What could replace it?
So we men know our place.
Beware of that sweet, smiling face,
So tender.
Why not surrender?
But as you feel her eyes taking command,

It's important that you understand,
Just out of sight,
She's holding tight
That apple firmly in her hand.

ONCE I WAS

I passed a graveyard, doubled back
And walked a thoughtful lonely track
Through sculpted headstones, in relief,
Imploring me
To feel their grief.
They beckoned me to stop and read
Their faded words, through tangled weed.
How many feet had passed them by
And missed the whisper....
"Here I lie."
Then under sullen, rain-filled skies,
I heard a thousand, silent cries -
"Pay heed to what you see because,
Like you I lived,
Once I was."
Why do we think that Father Time
Has no designs on yours or mine?
This uninvited guest will show
One day and say,
"It's time to go."
I left that place, my collar high
In driving rain, with sober eye,
To cherish every day, because
The hour would come

When once, I was.

SECURITY CONSCIOUS

You may bolt all your doors
As day turns into night
And keep all of your valuables
Padlocked out of sight.
And you may have a safe
Which you keep bolted to the floor.
If a burglar cannot lift it
Then he won't come back for more.
You may put your family jewels
In a strongbox, in a sack,
Hide it underneath the floorboards,
Then nail the floorboards back.
And any pocket change
You may secrete within
The confines of your kitchen,
In a biscuit tin.
Now, all of your belongings
Are secure as they may be.
They're bolted
And they're padlocked
And they're under lock and key.
But there is a treasured item
With which one day
You'd wish to part

Should someone special wish to steal it,
So don't lock up your heart.

PEARLY GATES

At the Pearly Gates, Peter
Looked sombre and grim.
"Whazza matter with your face?" I said,
"Let me in."
St. Peter looked sad
And just shook his head,
"You were bad enough down there,
You're as bad, now you're dead."
I poked at his chest
And I just told him straight,
"Don't give me your hassle, pal,
Open that gate.
If you know what's good for you,
Don't give me no grief,
If you mess me about
You'll have re-arranged teeth."
He made a small sign
With a very sad face
And I found myself in
A terrible place.
It's pretty hot down here,
No women, no beer
But at least I've got company -
My mates are all here.

PANDORA'S BOX

In the mists of our antiquity
Man dreamt of what could be.
We inherited his vision
In our mythology.
And on his journey through the ages
Man has found his way
To turn into reality
The dreams of yesterday.
We have rubbed Aladdin's lamp.
Our three wishes have been granted.
We have climbed the tree of knowledge
That our ancestors planted.
Now we have a thousand Babylons
And outsail Sinbad 'cross the seas.
We can split the atom
And make weapons of disease.
We reach out to the stars
To vie with Icarus.
We deep sea dive with Neptune,
We fly with Pegasus
But all of man's ambitions
Possess a counter force.
Beware of Greeks that bear you gifts.
Beware the Trojan horse.

For as man surfs the net
Every door unlocks
To all the good and evil
Within Pandora's box.

A GRAIN OF SAND

I raise my eyes to the night sky,
And I behold
A universe of secrets left untold
And Adam's moon bathes me in light,
As a shooting star takes flight
And a thousand constellations
Lend their glory to my sight.
In primal wonder I dare ask
Why should it be, that all the splendour
Of this world God gave to me?
But how am I to understand
With feeble skills at my command
For in this infinite creation
I am but a grain of sand.
Unto the stars, my insignificance is clear
And my cloak of self importance, a veneer.
Yet my inheritance from birth
Is to reign over this earth.
What gives a grain of sand called man
Such substance to his worth?
And introspection grants me guidance
From above
For when I close my eyes, I visualise
The symbol of the dove.

I find the answer that I seek.
I bow my head.
Man is unique.
For I was given the capacity
To love.

ANOTHER CLICHE

At the end of the day
It's just another cliché
And basically, I ask what can you do?
Is it because it's all the rage
Now in this day and age?
But if you ask me
I haven't got a clue.
So let me make it clear
The same old phrases re-appear.
24/7 and very much so,
They've had a good kick at the ball
And still they mean nothing at all.
But have a nice day or whatever.
There you go.
It keeps you on your toes.
But that's the way it goes.
It's the way the cookie crumbles.
That's a cert.
But they don't give you a prize for it
And that's about the size of it.
I've been there and I've got the tee shirt.
To let you understand
Things are getting out of hand.
So let me put you right, mind how you go.

I only play to win.
Just like it says on the tin.
And it takes one to know one, y'know.
So now we've chewed the fat
And you know where it's at.
The pen that I am holding is unsteady
Because, it may be just a hunch
But when it comes down to the crunch,
I think that I am missing you already.

HOLLY

They could take me to see
Many wonderful things,
Pyramids, towers and castles of kings,
The riches and treasures that all this world brings.
Then I'd know what they'd do,
Show me Buckingham Palace
And grand stately halls,
The power and spray of Victoria Falls,
The Australian bush
Where the wild dingo calls,
The Taj Mahal too,
Panoramas and vistas
And fabulous sights,
Tropical sunsets and Northern lights,
Safaris at dawn
And Parisienne nights
They'd bring to my view.
The Great Wall of China
I'd see from the skies
And above the Grand Canyon
I'd watch the sun rise.
But nothing they'd show me
Would pleasure my eyes
As when I see you.

WELL- BALANCED VIEW

A man walks through a field
And keeps looking down.
He's cursing at cow pats
And wearing a frown.
He's dodging each cow pat
Wherever they lie
But the fine summer day
Is passing him by.
The next man's a dreamer.
His head is held high.
He glories in sunshine,
The hills and blue sky.
He never looks down
Though maybe he should
And he leaves the field thinking
Something doesn't smell good.
The third man walks slowly
As he makes his way.
He warms to the sunshine
And smells new mown hay.
He notices cow pats
And passes them by
And hears the lark singing
In a lazy, blue sky.

He sees the whole picture
Unlike the other two
And he is the man
With the well-balanced view.

JIGSAW

When I was born, I had the basis
Of four corners
With nothing but a vacuum in between.
There was no guide for me to show
Where missing pieces had to go
Or what the final picture was to mean.
And as a young man, life had got so much
To show me
And temptation, joy and heartache
Came my way.
But with every lesson learned
Another piece was earned
And my jigsaw grew a little every day.
Yes, I was not immune to invitations
To wander off the straight and beaten track
And pieces would be lost
Until I stopped to count the cost,
Then I would find them
And would put the pieces back.
And maturity needs time to mend a fool.
But as I aged, I tried to walk within the light.
No longer did I try to fit
An errant, mis-shaped bit
For a piece was either wrong

Or it was right.
And now, tomorrows do not wait on my horizon
And my eyes are growing tired
My body weak.
But in this picture I have made
No conclusion is displayed
For it must need the missing piece,
Which I still seek.
And as my eye fades out of focus
For the last time
And my pulse can only offer one last beat,
I see a shining, loving face,
Put the final piece in place
And the jigsaw of my life
Is now complete.

PEOPLE AND ONIONS

If you have a dog,
Then you have a friend.
A dog will be loyal
And true to the end.
And to hear your cat purr,
Brings a smile to your eye.
Only people, and onions
Are what make you cry.
Whether you're smiling
Or wearing a frown,
The sun will come up
And the sun will go down.
On the cycle of nature
You can rely.
Only people and onions
Are what make you cry.
A river won't cheat you,
It just rolls along.
A lark won't deceive you,
She just sings her song.
The stars will shine on you
And tell you no lie.
Only people, and onions
Are what make you cry.

Some things you can depend on
Right from the start
That won't make you cry
And won't break your heart.
Now as I reflect
On the life that I've had,
I'm thinking that onions
Aren't really that bad.

FIRST THOUGHTS

I am, so I must be.
But who am I?
I think that I am me.
But don't know why
And if I am
Then I must be alive.
But how did I get here
And when did I arrive?
Where did I come from
And will I grow?
How can I find out
The things I need to know?
Who are these people
That I can see?
Why are they so big
Compared to me?
What are the answers
To it all?
I have big questions
Though I am small.
But for the moment
I know I am.
So now I'm going back to sleep
Inside my pram.

FAITH, HOPE AND CHARITY

Faith and hope and love
Are unique to every man.
To nourish and aspire to
Like no other species can.
Faith will give him purpose,
Hope the strength he needs
But blended with a loving heart,
He's truly blessed indeed.

The man with only hope
Has got no faith at all.
He backs off from relationships,
His heart behind a wall.
He smiles in any weather
Although the rain may pour.
His heart is full of hope
But what is he hoping for?
Perhaps to win the lottery
Or meet somebody new.
His hope will keep him going
But where is he going to?

The man with only faith
Can sometimes be severe.

He knows just where he's going
But there's little he holds dear.
He's pretty quick to criticise
And point out moral danger,
But he seldom holds a hand out
To help a passing stranger.
He believes in the hereafter
And spends much time in prayer
But without hope, for all his sins,
He's sure he won't get there.

And then there's love,
As we are told
The greatest of them all.
So great that it might stand alone
If faith and hope should fall.
This man sees the outstretched hand,
He takes it and holds tight.
This man says he's sorry
When he knows that he was right.
He sees others best points
Not dwelling on their worst.
He stands last and smiling
At others coming first.
He will grieve for others loss
And comfort where he may.
He is never wary of the price
That he may pay.
His loving heart is faithful

For as long as he may live.
His heart is never vengeful,
But ready to forgive.
And love without desire
Its purest form conveys
And manifests itself
In a myriad of ways.

For love is softly spoken.
Love is never loud.
Love is never envious.
Love is never proud.
Love is given freely.
It never seeks to gain.
Love is always in a heart
That feels another's pain.
For love is about giving
And never about take.
A giver warms the heart
A taker makes it break.

And you may make arrangements
In the twilight of your days
For all of your possessions
To divide in different ways.
And as that twilight darkens,
Your hope will keep you strong.
Your faith will give belief
You're going back where you belong.

But when your life has ended,
And you're laid into a grave,
The legacy that lingers on
Is all the love you gave.

LADY IN THE HOUSE
(for Ann)

I have a lady in the house
Imperious and royal
And I must be subservient
And dutiful and loyal.
And sometimes she'll communicate
With a short "meow",
Then I must work out what she wants
As I scrape and bow.
She maintains the highest standards
With a frequent wash and groom
To ensure that I appreciate
Her presence in the room.
She'll sit upon the window sill
And study every bird
But she doesn't care for dogs
In fact, she thinks they're quite absurd.
And if I have been good
As I stroke her fur,
She may choose to reward me
With a satisfactory purr.
She'll snuggle up beside me
When I'm on my own.
And I guess that she must love me
Since she lets me share her home.

THE GOOD OLD DAYS

Take me back to the good old days
When life was better in so many ways.
If you needed a servant or a kitchen maid
It was made so easy with the slavery trade.
The poor were no problem in the days of old
In a really bad winter they might die of cold.
But they knew what to do in the days of yore
They'd thin them down with another war.
If the right religion was the one you'd got
The king would slaughter all the other lot.
And the innocents took their statements back
Persuaded of their guilt with an hour on the rack.
And disease would keep the population down,
If someone sneezed, they'd wear a frown,
Look apprehensive, scared and vague,
Euthanasia was pointless
When they had the black plague.
Take me back to the days back when
The mentally ill didn't bother them.
They were not allowed to wander free.
They locked them up and threw away the key.
The entertainment was so good there
With public hangings in the market square.
On a Saturday night it was so much fun,

Take your granny and the kids along.
So take me back to ....
Take me back......
Take me, wait – I'm on the brink
It seems I'm having a re-think.
The good old days don't seem so dear
On second thoughts
I'll stay right here.

ANGEL
(for Isabel)

Stay close to me angel,
I know that you care.
I sense in my life
You have always been there.
When I was a baby,
Your face I could see
But as I got older
The world blinded me.
I need to say "sorry"
For the worry and pain
That I must have caused you
Time and again.
But whenever I stumbled
Off the right track,
I could feel angel's breath
Gently blowing me back.
I've heard you laugh with me
Together we've cried.
Each hour of my life
You've shared at my side.
Stay close, my dear angel
My days in the sun
Are dwindling fast.
Soon your work will be done.
And I know you'll be waiting

With the last breath I own,
To open your wings
And carry me home.

SANCTUARY

As summer sunset paints the sky aglow
And early evening shadows softly show,
I will suspend and leave behind
The tribulations of mankind.
To the sanctum of my garden I will go
And my spirit will discard it's cares and woes
And tranquility will grant my soul repose.
In healing silence I will rest
And my eyes will be caressed
By nature in her season's finest clothes.
Where the spindly seedlings grown from yesterday
Have become the fashion models of today
And they disdain all gaps and spaces
In their parade of festive faces
With all the colours of the rainbow on display.
A late night shopping bee's at work somewhere
And I trace his hyperactive buzz to where
From her deeply thorned defences,
A rose assails my senses
With the incense of her scent upon the air.
A butterfly will flutter into view
In bold designer costume, red and blue
And for a quarter of an hour,
She will flit from flower to flower

Seeking colours she can match her beauty to.
Then from his citadel atop a maple tree
A thrush will sing his goodnight song to me.
And the rustle of the leaves
Stirred by a gentle breeze
Accompany the maestro's rhapsody.
And as a crescent moon begins to rise
He takes his final bow and home he flies.
Then darkness will descend.
My time in sanctuary will end.
And I leave with peace rekindled in my eyes.

WINDOWS OF THE SOUL

The truth need not be spoken.
It is there to realise.
So much to learn of someone
Is written in their eyes.
If pretension seeks to charm
With flattery and guile,
The illusion is transparent
When the eyes forget to smile.
For a mother at the cradle
Or new husband with his bride
The look of love is unmistakable.
It has no place to hide.
The hooded eye remains half-closed
So it may not reveal
That the words its lips are speaking
Have something to conceal.
Yet the heart that speaks of love
In its earthly eye will show
The milk of human kindness
With a warm and tender glow.
But the eyes devoid of feeling
Betraying sin and vice,
Are the eyes lost to salvation
Encased in shards of ice

Each time we give of who we are
Outwith our control,
When we draw back the curtain
On the windows of our soul.

HOW ARE YOU?

I met a lady in the town
And she said, "How are you?'
I told her that I thought I might
Be coming down with flu.
More to the point, my lower back
Was playing up again
And that resulted from a fall
I'd had when I was ten.
And I'd seen my doctor twice that week
But he'd failed to diagnose
The agony that plagued me
In one of my big toes.
And I was having lots of trouble
With a temperamental tooth
With drinks or food too hot or cold
The pain went through the roof.
My blood pressure was stable
But I had no idea why
With the stress that I was under
It should have been sky-high.
And then I asked her, "How are you?"
Good manners so to keep
But I couldn't get an answer
As she seemed to be asleep.

A FATHER'S PRAYER

When they are small
Let me protect them.
Let those who wish them harm,
Beware.
Make them aware
They live in safety.
A father's strength
Is always there.
And as they grow
Let me be constant
In showing them
I care.
That when they fall
And they are crying,
A father's arms
Are always there.
Give me the grace
That I am mindful, as they learn
How they should live.
It's not the rulebook
That I give them
But the example
That I give.
And when they start

To make mistakes,
As they are surely
Bound to do,
Would you please
Remind me
That once,
I made them too.
And when they go
To lead their lives
And I sit in
My rocking chair.
Let them know,
If they should need me,
A father's love
Is always there.

MESSAGE TO OUTER SPACE

We send this CV
For you to appraise
To describe who we are
In a number of ways.
We killed off many species
For food or for fun
Until we evolved
To be the main one.
Our planet has riches
And plenty to spare.
But with the downtrodden,
We don't choose to share.
We could wipe out disease
And much suffering, but...
We don't put resources
Into that kind of thing.
So, our scientists build weapons
Of mass destruction instead,
Where one bomb can account for
Some ten thousand dead.
We readily breed
But as our numbers soar,
We have ethnic cleansing
Or just go to war.

So, we've come a long way,
I'm sure you'll agree.
And we're highly intelligent
As you can see.
So, let's get to the point
With no further fuss.
Our question is this:
Would you like to meet us?

A FRIEND IN NEED

"Life doesn't have a boy's gate.
Everyone has stormy weather.
Bite the bullet.
See a counsellor.
Pull yourself together.
You need to toughen up.
Everybody has ill health.
It's mind over matter.
Take a good look
At yourself.
Get a grip.
Have a break.
You've got too short a tether.
Only you can sort it out.
Pull yourself together."
"Well I'm so glad that we met.
I was having a bad day.
So I'll consider your advice
As I go along my way.
But your words, might hold more weight,
If, - to someone in a jam,
For just one milli-second,
You had shown
You gave a damn."

I WILL SERVE THE WINE

When I am king of everything
The crown jewels shall be sold
And all my court physicians
Will be sent on healing missions
To tend the sick
At cost of royal gold.
And my plethora of silk and satin garments
My men will take and go in search of those
Who live in squalor and starvation
In the back streets of my nation
And they will be the ones
To wear such clothes.
And for those who chose
To prey on the downtrodden
For their evil, from my kingdom shall be sent
And in exile, spend their days
To re-evaluate their ways
Until they seek forgiveness
And repent.
And my city gates will open
To the homeless,
Who for so long have been staring
At closed doors.
No longer will they be denied,

And as they step inside
They will hear a trumpet fanfare
And applause.
And for the needy and the poor
And the downhearted
There will be a banquet
Rich and fine.
They will have venison and cake,
And they will merry-make,
And I will lead the songs
And serve the wine.

ONE OF THOSE DAYS

You wake up in the morning
And you're lying in a haze.
You know before you get up
It'll be one of those days.
You cut yourself while shaving.
The sink is turning red
And in the bathroom mirror
There's a man who looks half-dead.
You cannot find a missing shoe
And hobble through the hall.
You trip over the missing shoe
And you bounce off the wall.
You need some toast and coffee
But you find you're out of bread
And the coffee jar is empty
So you kick the cat instead.
The cat is not too happy
And sticks out all its claws,
Straight into your ankle
And the neighbours hear your roars.
And why is it still dark outside?
You check your watch and scream.
You miss-set your alarm clock.
It's only three fifteen.

THE CHILD IN YOUR EYES

When you looked at me,
Something there I could see
Which hit me with total surprise.
At that moment I stole
A glimpse of your soul
When I saw the child in your eyes.
And I suddenly knew
It had to be you.
I would follow my heart where it flies.
No reflection or pause,
I knew I was yours
When I saw the child in your eyes.
And the years passed us by,
The years of you and I,
When you were my ultimate prize.
And all of the while,
I lived for that smile
And the love from the child in your eyes.
Then fate had it's way
Now I live out each day.
The past is where my future lies.
But if I count to ten.
I can dream of days when,
I was loved by the child in your eyes.

MY PRIZE

I don't have an Oscar
Or a V.C.
I did not win a Bafta
Or an O.B.E.
I've no golden disc
To hang on my wall.
No gold, bronze or silver
Sports medals at all.
I've no Wimbledon Trophy
And strangely to tell
I've been overlooked
By Alfred Nobel.
But I've seen a rainbow
Shimmer on high
And heard a lark singing
In a lazy blue sky.
And I've watched the sun rise
To vanquish the gloom
And smelled a red rose
When it's newly in bloom.
And I've seen my reflection
In my childrens' eyes
And I have been loved
And that is my prize.

BRAIN SCAN

Met this guy in the park
Who was down on his luck,
Who looked like he'd been hit
By a twenty ton truck.
He was dirty, unshaven,
His clothes a disgrace,
With deep sunken eyes
In a wrinkly face.

It started to rain
So due to the weather,
We had to take shelter
And sit there together.
Now I had to listen
To all of his stuff
About the last war
And how he'd had it rough.

Soon the rain stopped
And thank god I could leave.
Then something happened
That I just can't believe.
I turned back and gave him
What money I had,

And then walked away
Knowing I had gone mad.
I must go to the doc.
It's brain damage I fear.
I've no money for fags
And no money for beer.
I could ask for a brain scan.
If I'm ill, then I should.
But then why the hell
Am I feeling so good?

BROTHER ASS

Saint Francis called him Brother Ass.
I tend to call him me.
But on reflection, we are two
So I should call us we.
The fact is that I live inside him.
It's my job to teach and guide him.
From birth to death, there's no sabbatical
But Brother Ass is problematical.
On one hand he's my outer shell.
He carries me through life so well.
He lets me see, he lets me walk,
He lets me hear, he lets me talk,
He lets me smell, he lets me feel,
For minor hurts, he can self-heal.
If something's wrong, he gives me pain
To warn me – put it right again.
With organs deep inside him
So complex, truth to tell,
They have a million functions
To keep him feeling well.
He is in fact a masterpiece
Of heavenly creation,
Who keeps our brain informed
Of every good and bad sensation.

But there's a fundamental problem -
He's as basic as can be.
"Keep me well and happy"
Is all he asks of me.
But I share the same brain with him.
That's where I hang out
With something called a conscience
That he doesn't know about.
And together with this conscience
Intrinsic to this brain,
There is staggering potential
To reach a higher plane.
I use our brain for thinking
From cradle to the grave
Of what is wrong and what is right
And how I should behave.
I wrestle with morality
And do the best I can
With ethics and the principle
To love your fellow man
But all the time I'm ambushed
By his every basic whim
As far as he's concerned,
I should concentrate on him.
He wants to sleep
He wants to eat
He wants a cup of tea.
He must go to the toilet.
He thinks he's hurt his knee.

Once I gave him nicotine,
A big mistake of mine.
He really got to like it
Now he wants it all the time.
He's very fond of alcohol,
I give him one and then
He has no idea when to stop
And wants another ten
And as for sister asses,
He really thinks they're great.
He knows that they're essential
To his need to procreate.
I may be trying hard to ponder
The meaning of my life
While he's saying he's attracted
To the next door neighbour's wife.
He has no moral compass
And without me saying "no"
He'd be an alcoholic
Or a drugged-up gigolo.
But then, he can surprise me,
He can show such tenderness
Or use his strength to carry
A brother in distress.
I feel a teardrop in his eye
With a baby on his knee
But he'll fight like a lion
To keep it safe and free.
He's a paradox, a riddle,

Incapable of blame
But he's done everything
I asked him
And I love him just the same.
I think that I'm a spirit
What you might call a soul
And he's been my faithful servant,
As long as I controlled.
And when his days are ended
As end they surely must
I will go where I must go
And he will turn to dust.
But parting is sweet sorrow
And when that comes to pass
For all our time together,
I'll thank you brother ass.

MASTERMIND

There are fairies at the bottom of my garden
And with my telescope
I watch them play at night.
And the pixies dance about
As they chase a goblin out
But they always disappear at morning light.
I would dearly love to travel round the world
But I'm far too scared
To take a chance on that.
For each and every year
Ships and planes just disappear
And it's clear that is because
The earth is flat.
I saw Elvis in a pet shop buying cat food.
So I asked if I could have an autograph
But I was quick to realise
That he was in disguise
So I didn't take offence when he just laughed.
There are those who think that I might be misguided
And they point at me
Wherever I may go.
But I laugh up my sleeve
For they only self-deceive
There are lots of things I know

That they don't know.
I know Egyptian pyramids
Were built by Martians
And a giant squid made the Titanic sink
And U.F.O's are coming soon
From the dark side of the moon
And I fully understand
How women think.

FAMOUS LAST WORDS

And now I say "Goodbye"
As the pulse dies in my wrist.
Maybe soon, they'll all appreciate
How much I will be missed.
I'm on my way to heaven,
Where the decent people go.
So sadly, we won't meet again
Since you'll be down below.
I can't say that I'm sorry
To leave this world behind.
With sinners all around me
I had no peace of mind.
I've been proper, I've been righteous
As every man should be
And there'll be a special welcome
For someone such as me.
I have led a life of virtue
And it's a certain bet,
I'll thoroughly deserve
The judgment that I get.
Now I'm at the Pearly gates
Where St. Peter meets the dead,
He's made a shocking error
He closed the gates and shook his head!

EUREKA

When it comes to the crunch,
It's a stone in the ground.
A pebble that glitters
And is seldom found.
You can smelt it or melt it,
Make bracelets or rings.
It's been used to create
Many bright, shiny things.
And of all of the stones
That lie in this earth,
Man has placed on it
A fabulous worth.
History shows us
Men have been turned mad
And deserted their loved ones
When there's gold to be had.
They've dug into mountains
And panned every stream,
Lost their minds and their lives
To fulfill their gold dream.
But who credited gold
With the value it's got?
Who held up a pebble
Saying, "It's worth a lot."

And we followed like sheep
In a blindfolded row,
Saying, "This must be precious
Because he said so!"
It's a pebble that glitters,
And although seldom found,
When it comes to the crunch,
It's just a stone in the ground.

THINGS

In the beginning I had nothing,
Nothing was what I had.
But I had love and I had laughter
So nothing wasn't bad.
But then I worked and I bought something
And owning something felt quite good.
Most people still had nothing
In my neighbourhood.
And I found when I had one thing
For me that would not do.
There always was another thing
That I needed too.
I became a businessman
And gave out orders everyday
And slowly, anything I wanted
Began to come my way.
And the harder that I worked,
The more money that would bring,
Until one day I concluded
That I had everything.
I had my cars and fashion clothes,
A country house and diamond rings,
Antique clocks and Persian carpets,
So many precious things.

But now I look at all my things
And they look back at me,
And I am deafened by a silence
Of soulless apathy.
And to those days when I had nothing
My heart has taken wings,
To live again with love and laughter
I would surrender all my things.

REMEMBER ME

Remember me when you are sleeping
And in the mantle of the night,
I will come to you and hold you safe
And make your fears take flight.
Remember me when you are weeping
Afraid your wounded heart might break,
That stony path I will walk with you
For every step you take.
Remember me when you are laughing
As sunlight shines on you,
For in the echo of your laughter
You will hear me laughing too.
Remember me when you are weary
And your spirit's strength is gone.
I will whisper words to raise you up
And help you journey on.
And should your final hours be lonely
With no comfort at your side,
Remember me, I will be waiting
With my arms open wide.

I AM MAN

I am Adam.
He was me.
We bear the same identity
And if he cost me paradise
That guilt is mine
We share the price.
This world is mine
To dominate,
To speak of love
Or preach of hate
And I have the capacity
To sink into depravity.
But where my spirit soars
And flies,
God is reflected
In my eyes.
This short life
Is a battlefield
Where I must fight
And must not yield
To forces that I cannot see
Who prize my soul
And covet me.
For I have fallen once before

And lost the key
To Eden's door.
And when I'm called
To heaven's gate
And for my second chance, I wait,
Contrite tears
My eyes will blind
For all the souls
Of humankind.
When angels whisper,
Is that him,
Sent from the Garden for his sin?
I'll tell them
That is who I am.
I am Adam.
I am man.

WITHOUT YOU

A nightingale without a song
Crossroads without a sign
Rain without a rainbow
A verse without a rhyme.
Autumn without falling leaves
A kiss without consent
A violin without a bow
A rose without a scent.
A garden without flowers
A sea without a shore
A door without a key
A key without a door.
A sonata without melody
A mountain top without a view
Christmas with no Santa Claus
As I am without you.

POET'S BLOCK

I thought I'd write a poem
But I really got a shock,
I found that I'd developed
Something called a block for poets.
It's similar to writers' block
But this could make me cry,
I can't get words to rhyme at all
No matter how I make an effort.
It really should be simple,
Instead of this heartache,
To rhyme two lines together
Should be a piece of bread.
And this is not improving,
It's going from worse to bad,
If this does not get better
It's sure to drive me insane.
I think that I might shoot myself,
But I don't have a gun
And you've got to keep on trying
When all is said and bottom line.
I took a break for half and hour
Then gave it one last try
But if I could get two words to rhyme
Then maybe pigs could swim.

I've had my fill of poetry
It's over, I am done.
And that is sure to bring relief
To each and every person.

Printed in Great Britain
by Amazon